ANIMAL LIVES

Mammals

WORLD BOOK

a Scott Fetzer company

Chicago

www.worldbookonline.com

World Book, Inc.
233 N. Michigan Avenue
Chicago, IL 60601
U.S.A.

For information about other World Book publications, visit our Web site at **http://www.worldbookonline.com** or call **1-800-WORLDBK (967-5325)**.

For information about sales to schools and libraries, call **1-800-975-3250 (United States)**, or **1-800-837-5365 (Canada)**.

Editorial:
Editor in Chief: Paul A. Kobasa
Project Manager: Cassie Mayer
Writer: Brian Johnson
Researcher: Jacqueline Jasek
*Manager, Contracts & Compliance
 (Rights & Permissions):* Loranne K. Shields
Indexer: David Pofelski

Graphics and Design:
Manager: Tom Evans
*Coordinator, Design Development
 and Production:* Brenda B. Tropinski
Book design by: Don Di Sante
Photographs Editor: Kathy Creech
Senior Cartographer: John Rejba

Pre-Press and Manufacturing:
Director: Carma Fazio
Manufacturing Manager: Steven K. Hueppchen
Senior Production Manager: Jan Rossing

Picture Acknowledgments:

Front Cover: © Anup Shah, Nature Picture Library/Minden Pictures; Back Cover: © AfriPics/Alamy Images

© Arco Images/Alamy Images 10; © blickwinkel/Alamy Images 16; © Brandon Cole Marine Photography/Alamy Images 37; © Bryan & Cherry Alexander Photography/Alamy Images 39; © Danita Delimont/Alamy Images 26-27; © Elvele Images/Alamy Images 39; © Michael Freeman, Alamy Images 26; © Nick Greaves, Alamy Images 8-9; © David Klein, Alamy Images 11; © Kuttig - People/Alamy Images 4; © Mark Levy, Alamy Images 27; © Robert McGouey, Alamy Images 15; © Inga Spence, Alamy Images 17; © Stock Connection Blue/Alamy Images 36; © Dan Sullivan, Alamy Images 32; © tbkmedia/Alamy Images 31; © Dave Watts, Alamy Images 13; © WaterFrame/Alamy Images 21; © Petra Wegner, Alamy Images 19; © Nigel Dennis, ABPL/Animals Animals 7; © Michael Habicht, Animals Animals 21, 30-31; © Breck P. Kent, Animals Animals 24; © Lightwave Photography/Animals Animals 7; © Peter Lilja, Animals Animals 31; © Michael Francis Photography/Animals Animals 22-23; © Mary Rhodes, Animals Animals 8; © Charles R. Smith, Animals Animals 30; © Stouffer Productions/Animals Animals 25; © Margie Wagner, Animals Animals 18-19; © Richard Alan Wood, Animals Animals 27; AP/Wide World 35; © Theo Allofs, Photonica/Getty Images 6; © John Downer, Taxi/Getty Images 12; © Thorsten Milse, Robert Harding World Imagery/Getty Images 43; © Michael Nichols, National Geographic/Getty Images 4-5; © Keren Su, Getty Images 40; © Peter Andrews, Reuters/Landov 41; © Finbarr O'Reilly, Reuters/Landov 43; © Zoom/Landov 40; © Suzi Eszterhas, Minden Pictures 29; © Konrad Wothe, Minden Pictures 33; © Christophe Courteau, Nature Picture Library 20-21; © Shutterstock 6, 13, 14, 24, 28, 29, 34, 42, 44, 45; © age fotostock/SuperStock 10, 14, 16, 19, 22, 23, 36-37, 38; © Photononstop/SuperStock 32; © Stockbyte/SuperStock 20

All maps and illustrations are the exclusive property of World Book, Inc.

Library of Congress Cataloging-in-Publication Data

Mammals / World Book.
   p. cm. -- (Animal lives)
  Includes index.
  Summary: "An introduction to mammals and their physical characteristics, life cycle, behaviors, and adaptations to various habitats. Features include maps, diagrams, fun facts, glossary, resource list, and index"--Provided by publisher.
  ISBN 978-0-7166-0406-8
  1. Mammals--Juvenile literature. I. World Book, Inc.
QL706.2.M28 2009
599--dc22
            2009008852

Animal Lives
Set ISBN: 978-0-7166-0401-3

Printed in China
1 2 3 4 5 13 12 11 10 09

Table of Contents

There is a glossary of terms on page 46. Terms defined in the glossary are in type **that looks like this** on their first appearance on any spread (two facing pages).

What Are Mammals?

What do cats, dogs, rabbits, and squirrels have in common? These animals seem very different from each other, but they all belong to the same animal group. They are called mammals. Most farm animals are mammals, including cows, goats, hogs, and horses. Unusual animals like anteaters, giraffes, kangaroos, and panda bears are mammals, too. The most familiar animal of all is a mammal: that's a human being like you!

Creature features

There are many different kinds of mammals, but they all have certain features in common. For example, all mammals are **vertebrates** (animals with backbones). All mammal young feed on their mother's milk. Mammals have some other features that make them different from other animals. You can read about these features on pages 6-7.

Where in the world?

There are more than 4,500 **species** (kinds) of mammals, and they can be found all around the world. Mammals like elephants and lions live in hot, tropical areas near the **equator.** Caribou, arctic foxes, and polar bears live in cold **polar regions.** Some mammals, like camels, live in deserts. Others swim in the ocean. One group of mammals, the bats, can even fly through the air. Mammals are often the largest animals in the places where they live.

Some of the most familiar animals are mammals, including dogs and even human beings.

Fun Fact

Mammals come in all sizes. The smallest mammal is Kitti's hog-nosed bat. It weighs about the same as a paper clip (1.5 grams). The largest animal that has ever lived is the blue whale. It weighs about 300,000 pounds (about 136,000 kilograms)!

Many mammals live together in groups, like these African baboons.

The balance of nature

Living things depend on mammals to help maintain the balance of nature. Mammals that eat fruits leave seeds in their droppings. These seeds may then sprout into new plants. Mammals that dig into the ground help keep the soil healthy for plants. Hunting mammals like wolves feed on plant-eaters like deer. This keeps the number of deer under control, so they don't eat all the plants. Otherwise, some plants would become extinct (gone forever). Mammals help keep **habitats** (places where plants and animals live) healthy for all living things.

What Are Features of Mammals?

Every kind of mammal has certain features that help it survive in its **habitat.** For example, giraffes are mammals that have long necks, which helps them reach the leaves of trees. But all mammals have certain features or traits in common.

Young mammals feed on their mother's milk, helping them grow big and strong.

Mammal young

One of the most important differences between mammals and other animals is how they produce and raise their young. Most mammals give birth to live young. Many other animals, like birds and **reptiles,** lay eggs. Mammal mothers also nurse their babies on their milk. This provides young mammals with just the right kind of food to help them grow.

Hairy bodies

Another characteristic of mammals is that they grow hair. Hair helps mammals survive in many different ways. The thick hair on a polar bear keeps it warm in the cold. The striped hairs on a tiger give it **camouflage** to help it blend in with its surroundings. Special hairs called quills are prickly to the touch. Quills protect porcupines from being eaten.

A tiger's tan fur and dark stripes help it blend in with its surroundings.

Temperature control

All mammals are **warm-blooded.** This means that their body temperature stays about the same no matter what the temperature is outside. Some animals

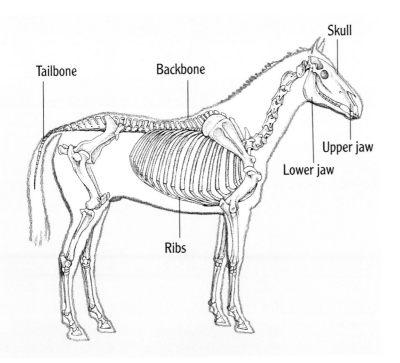

Tailbone Backbone Skull

Upper jaw

Lower jaw

Ribs

All mammals have backbones and strong skeletons. Mammals like horses gallop quickly on their four legs.

that are not mammals, like birds, are also warm-blooded. Other creatures, like snakes and other **reptiles,** are not. Reptiles cannot live in cold places because they would freeze to death.

Big brains!

Many mammals have larger, more complex brains than other animals. This allows them to learn. Dolphins, dogs, and chimpanzees are among the smartest animals. Human beings have the most complex brains of all.

Most mammals protect their young for longer periods than other animals do, giving young mammals time to learn from their parents. Human children stay with their parents for a long time, learning all they need to know.

All mammals grow hair. Sea otters stay warm in the water with thick coats of fur.

What Senses Do Mammals Have?

Mammals use many different senses to learn about their surroundings. The major senses mammals use are smell, taste, hearing, sight, and touch.

Elephants smell and touch using their amazing trunks. Their large ears help them hear sounds.

Smell

For most mammals, smell is the most important sense. They use it to find food and avoid **predators** (hunting animals). Many mammals also use smell to communicate. For example, dogs urinate on trees to mark their **territory**. When a dog smells a tree, it learns about all the dogs that have urinated there. Some mammals have an incredibly powerful sense of smell. Bloodhounds are dogs that can smell that a person ran through the woods even days later!

Taste

Mammals use their tongues to taste the world around them. The sense of taste helps mammals tell if something might be good to eat.

Hearing

The sense of hearing is important for many mammals. They are the only animals with an outer ear, which helps them listen to faint or distant sounds. Zebras can turn their outer ears to focus on certain sounds. If a lion sneaking up on a zebra makes the slightest sound, the zebra's ears may turn toward the sound to sense if there is danger.

Many mammals have excellent eyesight. An owl monkey's large eyes help it see well at night.

Sight

Sight is the most important sense for some mammals, including human beings. People can see colors, but most mammals are color-blind. Mammals that are **nocturnal,** like the owl monkey, often have large eyes to help them see in the dark.

Touch

Touch is an important sense for many mammals. Mammals with whiskers can feel their way in the dark. For example, cats can find mice at night by sensing tiny movements of air with their whiskers.

Fun Fact

Some mammals use their sense of hearing to "see" with sound. This is called **echolocation.** Mammals like bats and dolphins make high-pitched sounds. The sound waves bounce off objects, producing echoes. These echoes tell the distance and direction to the objects.

What Do Mammals Eat?

A mammal's diet can depend largely on where the animal lives. Some mammals eat only plants, and some eat only meat. Others, like human beings, eat plants and meat. Mammals often have special **adaptations** that make them especially suited to their diet. Adaptations are features that help an animal survive.

A giraffe's long neck and tongue allow it to eat leaves growing on tall trees.

Plant-eaters

Most mammals eat plants. Plant-eating mammals have special teeth, because tough plants would quickly wear down ordinary teeth. Some mammals, like cattle, elephants, and horses, have teeth that rise far into the gums. These teeth provide extra material for wear and tear. Mammals like mice and rats have special front teeth that grow throughout their lives, like fingernails.

Like many predators, lions have long canine teeth that they use to pierce the flesh of prey.

Meat-eaters

Other mammals are **predators** that hunt for food. Mammals that eat animal flesh have long, pointed canine teeth near the front of the mouth. These teeth help them to catch, hold, and pierce the flesh of their **prey** (animals that are hunted). Mammals like leopards, lions, and wolves bite off large chunks of meat that they swallow without chewing. Dolphins use their special cone-shaped teeth to catch and hold fish, which they swallow whole.

Scavengers

Some mammals are **scavengers.** They feed on the remains of dead animals. Hyenas are scavengers that use their powerful jaws to crush and eat the bones of animal remains.

Insect-eaters

Some of the most unusual mammals are insect-eaters, like the giant anteater. Giant anteaters have no teeth. Instead, they lick up ants and termites with their long tongues.

Everything on the menu

Certain other mammals eat both animals and plants. These mammals have teeth designed to grind up plants *and* tear off flesh. Bears, hogs, opossums, and raccoons are plant- and meat-eaters. Many human beings are, too!

Fun Fact Some animals change their diet with the seasons. For example, spotted skunks are mammals that eat mainly seeds, fruit, and insects in the summer. During winter, they eat mainly mice and rats.

Bears eat both plants and animals. This brown bear has caught a tasty salmon from an Alaskan river.

How Do Mammals Grow?

Mammals go through different stages of development called the **life cycle.** For a mammal, life begins inside its mother's body. Most mammals give birth to young that have grown for a long time inside the mother.

Development

Mammals grow and develop at different rates. A gerbil is born after about a month inside its mother. Human beings are born after about 9 months. Killer whales are born after about 17 months!

Cheetah cubs stay with their mother for a long time after they are born, drinking milk and learning how to hunt.

Small mammals, like mice and shrews, often leave their mothers when they no longer need milk. Larger mammals, like cheetahs and elephants, often stay even after they stop drinking milk. Staying with their mother gives young mammals more time to learn how to survive.

Life span

Mammals differ in how long they live. Most mice live for 2 years or less. Elephants can live about 65 years. Human beings can live more than 100 years. The bowhead whale can live more than 200 years!

Marsupials

One kind of mammal must leave the inside of its mother's body when it is still extremely small and frail. These mammals are called **marsupials.** Kangaroos, the koala, and possums are marsupials. Marsupials grow for only 7 to 14 days before they must crawl out and make their way to the mother's pouch. In the pouch, young marsupials drink milk and continue to grow. They usually stay inside the mother's pouch for several months.

Young kangaroos are born when they are still young and frail. They finish growing in their mother's pouch.

Do Mammals Build Homes?

Many mammals do not build homes. Instead, they simply sleep on the ground. Some land mammals, like cows, sleep standing up. Some ocean mammals, like dolphins and whales, can sleep underwater. But other mammals build shelters where they can rest, raise their young, or hide from **predators**.

Every night, chimpanzees build new nests in the trees, giving them a place to sleep.

Temporary homes

Some mammals build temporary homes each night. When it's time go to sleep, chimpanzees make a nest out of tree branches and leaves. In the morning, they leave behind their nests to start a new day.

Underground homes

Some mammals build long-lasting homes for shelter. Many smaller mammals dig **burrows** (underground homes) that they live in for most of their lives. Chipmunks, gophers, meerkats, and rabbits all dig burrows. Burrows offer mammals protection from harsh weather and provide a place for them to hide from predators.

Unique homes

A few mammals spend much of their time gathering material to build large homes. Beavers have strong, sharp teeth that they use to gnaw through trees. After the trees fall, beavers strip away the branches and the bark. They use the fallen trees to build dams. Some beaver dams measure more than 1,000 feet

Many smaller mammals like this meerkat dig underground burrows, with many ways in and out.

Beavers use their strong, sharp teeth to gnaw through trees, *right*. They gather branches to build special dens, *above*. These dens are called beaver lodges.

(305 meters) long! Beavers also use fallen trees to build special dens called lodges. Beavers usually build lodges on the water. A lodge resembles a teepee that rises 3 to 6 feet (0.9 to 1.8 meters) above the water. Each lodge has several underwater entrances, which makes it difficult for predators to get inside. In their lodges, beavers give birth, raise their young, and huddle together to stay warm.

Fun Fact

Burrows can be very large with many ways to get in and out. An Australian **marsupial** called the boodie digs burrows with as many as 90 different entrances!

Do Mammals Live in Groups?

Some mammals live in groups for much of their lives, but others live alone. Solitary and group life offer different benefits for mammals.

Wolves live together in large groups called packs. Wolf packs hunt together and share their kills.

Mammal loners

Some mammals spend most of their lives alone. Leopards, tigers, and most other cats get together only to **reproduce** (make more of themselves). It is easier for these **predators** to sneak up on **prey** when they are alone. When they do make a catch, they don't have to share their food!

Just a few of us

Some mammals live together in small groups, which might include only an adult male, an adult female, and their young. Beavers are mammals that live in such groups.

Mammals like the American badger spend most of their lives alone.

Big families

Other mammals live in large groups. Horses and seals form groups that have one adult male and several adult females, along with their young. The male is the father of all the females' young. Other mammals live in groups with several males and females.

Large groups are often organized by rank (social position). Baboons, rhesus monkeys, and wolves all live in groups with rank. Members of a group may fight to establish rank, but they rarely harm each other.

Members with higher rank often get the best food. For example, when wolves kill a caribou, the highest-ranking members get their choice of the meat. Rank also has an effect on how much an animal may reproduce. High-ranking males in rhesus monkey groups usually father the most young.

Why live in groups?

Group life helps mammals survive. Predators like killer whales, lions, and wolves all hunt in groups. The group works together to attack prey. Other mammals live in groups for protection. Members of the group can warn others of danger. For example, if one white-tailed deer senses danger, it can warn other deer by flashing the white underside of its tail. When a group runs, it is hard for predators to know which animal to chase.

A group of horses has many eyes to watch for predators. Horses in the herd compete for rank.

Are Mammals Territorial?

Many mammals claim a **territory** (area of land) to help them meet their food needs and to attract mates (partners). Individuals often get into fights with other members of their **species** to defend their territory.

Fighting over females

Some mammals claim territories during mating, when males try to attract females so they can produce young. Males with the best territory are more likely to be chosen as mates, so they often fight to claim and protect their territory.

Male northern elephant seals have fierce fights over territory. Every summer, the seals crowd onto islands in the Pacific Ocean to prepare for the mating season. On the islands, the males fight with each other to claim a territory. Males that claim the best areas of beach are the most successful at attracting females.

Protecting food supplies

Many other mammals claim territories to protect their food supply. Apes called gibbons live in Asian tropical rain forests. There is only so much of the fruit and leaves for gibbons to eat in an area of forest, so gibbon groups claim a territory to prevent other gibbons from taking their food.

The amount of food available often determines a territory's size. For example, if an area has plenty of food, a wolf territory may be as small as 30 square miles (78 square kilometers). If there is little food

Male elephant seals fight for territory during the mating season. The fights are fierce but rarely cause serious injury.

Gibbons claim territory with loud hoots that carry through the forest.

in an area, the territory may cover 800 square miles (2,100 square kilometers).

Marking territory

Mammals have different ways of keeping others from entering their territory. Male gibbons warn animals away by singing songs and making loud calls. Wolves urinate on rocks, trees, and other objects to mark the border lines of their territory. House cats have special **glands** in their cheeks that produce smelly oils. They rub their cheeks on objects to mark them with the oil. People can't smell the oil, but it warns other cats to keep their distance.

Cats rub their cheeks on objects in their territory, leaving behind an oil that other cats can smell.

How Do Mammals Hunt and Escape?

Impalas try to escape predators like cheetahs by running at great speed.

Many mammals hunt other animals for food. Others, such as plant-eaters or small mammals, must try to hide or escape from **predators.**

Fierce predators

Some mammals have bodies built for hunting. A tiger has teeth as long as 3 inches (7.6 centimeters) and claws that can reach 5 inches (12.7 centimeters) long—almost half the length of a ruler! While walking, a tiger keeps its claws pulled back in a protective covering so they stay especially sharp.

Solitary hunters

Some mammals hunt alone so they can sneak up on their **prey.** Many of these mammals have fur that **camouflages** the animal. Their fur may have special markings or simply be the same color as their surroundings. When these predators get close enough, they make a final dash at high speed to catch their prey.

Skunks scare predators away by spraying a foul-smelling liquid at them.

Group hunters

Other mammals hunt in groups. Dolphins work together to herd fish into a small group so they are easier to catch. Wolves take turns chasing their prey until they wear it out. Lions often set traps. One lion may startle a zebra into running toward other lions that are hiding in the grass.

Time to flee!

To escape predators, many mammals depend on their speed. Most hoofed mammals, like deer and impalas (an African antelope), can run at great speed over long distances. This wears out predators, who may give up the chase.

Small mammals, like chipmunks and prairie dogs, often escape predators by diving into their **burrows.** Squirrels and monkeys escape by climbing trees. Other mammals may escape predators by remaining perfectly still. A rabbit that freezes may be hard to see.

Some mammals have unique defenses. The hard plates of armadillos are hard to pierce. Porcupines have sharp, stiff quills that keep predators away. Skunks spray a foul-smelling liquid at predators. Once sprayed, a predator is unlikely to bother skunks again!

Fun Fact

When threatened, American opossums go completely limp. Many predators lose interest in prey that seems dead. Pretending to be dead is sometimes called "playing possum."

Dolphins work together to herd sardines, making the fish easier to catch.

Do Mammals Migrate?

Many mammals **migrate,** or travel from one area to another. Mammals migrate to find the best food, to avoid harsh weather, to give birth, or to do all three.

Winter migration

Many mammals migrate to warmer **climates** to avoid winter, when little food is available. North American bats that feed on insects migrate southward each autumn because there are few insects around during the cold northern winter. When spring begins to arrive in North America, they make the trip back north.

Grassland migrations

In central Africa, wildebeests and zebras migrate during the dry season in search of green grass. About 1.5 million wildebeest and more than 200,000 zebras migrate across hundreds of miles.

In Africa, wildebeests and zebras wade across dangerous rivers in search of fresh grass.

Fun Fact

A large North American deer called the caribou makes the longest land migration of any animal. Some caribou migrate more than 3,000 miles (4,800 kilometers)!

American elk migrate down into mountain valleys to avoid harsh winter weather.

Mountain migrations

American elk (a type of deer) live high in the mountains during summer. In the winter, mountains become extremely cold, and heavy snowfall makes it difficult to graze on plants or even to move. To avoid these conditions, American elk migrate down into the valleys, where the weather is not as harsh.

Ocean migrations

Every fall, gray whales swim from the Arctic Ocean to the warmer seas off the western coast of Mexico to give birth. There is little or no food for the whales in these waters. The whales make the trip because newborn whales could not survive the freezing temperatures in the Arctic.

In the southern waters, the adult whales live off the fat that they built up during the summer. The newborn whales drink their mother's milk while they grow. By the time the whales return to the Arctic, the young whales have grown enough to survive the cold.

Gray whales migrate from Arctic to Mexican waters to give birth to young.

Do Mammals Hibernate?

When winter comes around, mammals must find a way to survive with little food available. Some mammals **migrate** to warmer places. Others go into a deep sleep called **hibernation**. During this period, their heartbeat and breathing become much slower. Their body temperature also falls, and they can't be awakened easily.

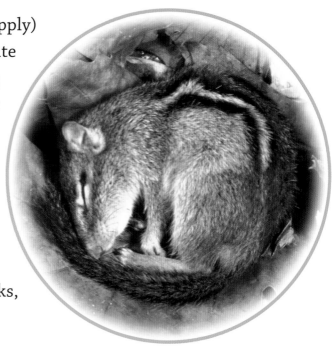

Many bats hibernate in caves during the winter, when there are few insects to eat.

Storing up for winter

In many places, food becomes scarce (in short supply) during winter months. So mammals that hibernate eat as much as they can during summer, building up fat. By hibernating, mammals use up their fat as slowly as possible. Their bodies need little energy to stay alive. If they stayed active, the mammals might not have enough fat to last through the winter.

Small hibernators

Many smaller mammals, including bats, chipmunks, marmots (a type of squirrel), and woodchucks, hibernate. Many rodents hibernate, too. These mammals usually dig a **burrow** where they can sleep safely through the winter. Burrows prevent the mammals from becoming too cold.

Small mammals like this chipmunk sleep through the winter in comfy burrows.

Bear hibernations

Bears that live in areas with cold winters often hibernate. Some bears dig holes so they can hibernate underground. Others make do with dens they find. They may hibernate under large rock formations, under tree roots, or in caves. The body temperature of hibernating bears does not fall as much as it does in smaller mammals.

Bears spend the summer building up fat, often by eating lots of fish like salmon. When bears awake from hibernation in the spring, they have gone from fat to skinny, and they are ready to eat!

Bears hibernate through the winter in their dens, surviving on fat stored up in the summer.

Fun Fact

Some mammals experience a kind of hibernation to avoid extreme heat. Certain kinds of bats and rodents that live in the desert become inactive during the hottest, driest part of the summer.

What Mammals Live in Forests?

Many kinds of mammals live in forest **habitats.**
A habitat is the kind of place where a plant or animal lives. The trees in forests provide shelter from harsh weather and from the sun. Trees provide food in the form of leaves, bark, nuts, and fruit.

Life in the trees

Many mammals have special **adaptations** for living in forests. Adaptations are features of an animal that help it survive. Many forest animals have adaptations that help them climb trees.

Apes and monkeys are often expert tree climbers. Orangutans are apes that have long, powerful arms with hook-shaped hands to help them swing from branch to branch. Many kinds of monkeys have tails that can grasp branches or other objects.

In South America, an unusual kind of mammal called the sloth hangs from branches using its hooklike claws. Sloths can hang from branches with so little effort that they even sleep that way.

Sloths use their hooklike claws to hang from branches.

Orangutans use their long arms and legs to move from branch to branch.

Squirrels also live in trees. A squirrel's long, bushy tail helps it to keep its balance as it leaps from tree to tree. Flying squirrels have flaps of skin between their front and back legs. These squirrels can't really fly, but they glide over long distances. They are held up in the air like a kite by the flaps of skin.

Flying squirrels glide between the trees using the flaps of skin between their legs.

Flying mammals

Bats are the only mammals that can fly. Many bats live in forests, where they usually feed on fruit or insects. Bats use their strong, handlike feet to hang upside down from trees or cave ceilings while resting. They hunt at night using **echolocation** to "see" in the dark.

Forest hunters

Many mammals that are **predators** live in forests. Most tigers live in forests, as do many other cats. Leopards sometimes attack from trees. They use their strong teeth to carry animals weighing as much as 150 pounds (68 kilograms) up into the tree!

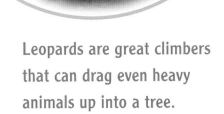

Leopards are great climbers that can drag even heavy animals up into a tree.

What Mammals Live in Grasslands?

Grasslands are flat, open areas with few trees. Large herds of mammals graze on plants in grassland **habitats**. These mammals must stay alert or they will become a tasty meal for nearby **predators**.

Bison use their great size and sharp horns to keep predators at a distance.

Making a quick getaway

Grasslands are filled with grazing mammals, such as antelopes, bison (wild oxen), cattle, horses, wildebeests, and zebras. Many of these mammals **migrate** long distances to reach the best food. Predators often follow these animals, waiting for the right time to attack. Because grasslands are open, animals that run at great speed may escape predators.

Zebras stare out over the open grassland, turning their ears toward any hint of danger.

Safety in numbers

Forming herds (groups) is another **adaptation** suited to grasslands. Mammals in herds have more sets of eyes and ears to watch for predators. When a herd runs, it can be hard for predators to track a single animal, especially for animals with **camouflage,** such as a zebra's stripes.

Fun Fact

Some plant-eaters in grasslands eat leaves rather than grass. Giraffes are the tallest animals, sometimes reaching more than 19 feet (5.8 meters) tall. Their long necks help them reach leaves high in the trees.

Grassland predators

Large cats are the top predators in many grassland habitats. In African grasslands, lions work together in groups called prides to hunt their **prey.** Cheetahs also live in African grasslands. They can outrun even the fastest prey, sprinting at 68 miles (110 kilometers) per hour. In the grasslands of South America, jaguars are the top predators.

Grasslands are also home to **scavengers,** such as hyenas and wild dogs called jackals. These animals eat the remains of dead animals that they find. They also hunt for food.

Hyenas are both hunters and scavengers. Their powerful jaws can crush bones, which the hyenas eat.

Grassland giants

Some grassland mammals depend on their size to protect them. A rhinoceros may weigh 3.5 tons (3.2 metric tons). Elephants may weigh more than 7 tons (6.4 metric tons). Both animals have thick, tough skin that is difficult for predators to pierce.

What Mammals Live on Mountains?

The mountains provide a home for many mammals, but life in the mountains can be hard. Steep slopes make it difficult for animals to move from one place to another. The temperature is also colder at higher elevations (heights). Winters can be especially harsh in the mountains, and many mountain peaks remain icy even in the summer.

Mountain goats live high in the mountains, climbing cliffs too steep for most predators.

Warm winter coats

Mammals that live on mountains have special **adaptations** to help them survive. Some mountain mammals have long hair with a thick undercoat to keep them warm. Many mammals also **migrate** to lower parts of the mountain when winter arrives.

Feet made for climbing

Some adaptations help mammals move along steep slopes without falling. Mountain goats have hard hoofs with sharp edges for cutting through ice. Their hoofs also have inner pads that grip slippery surfaces.

Small mountain mammals

Many rodents and rabbits live in the mountains. Some rodents, like marmots, **hibernate** during the coldest months. Other animals, like mountain hares, do not hibernate. With little food available for **predators,** mountain hares are often hunted. But they have a unique adaptation to help them hide. They turn white in the winter, which provides **camouflage** in the snow.

Mountain predators

Predators like large cats also live in the mountains. Snow leopards climb to amazing heights in the world's highest mountain ranges in Asia. Their long tails and broad paws help them creep along steep slopes.

Mountain lions are big cats that live in the mountains of North and South America. They use their long back legs to jump as far as 40 feet (12.2 meters) to catch **prey.**

Mountain lions use their powerful legs to leap on prey like deer and mountain goats.

Pikas are close relatives of rabbits. They live on mountains, where they spend much of their time gathering food for winter.

Fun Fact

A kind of monkey called the Japanese macaque *(muh KAHK)* lives in the mountains of Japan. It stays warm in the winter by relaxing in volcanic hot springs—nature's version of the hot tub!

What Mammals Live in Deserts?

Deserts are dry regions that receive little rainfall. During the day, temperatures often reach 100 °F (38 °C) or more. At night, temperatures plunge to near freezing. Few plants and animals can survive these extreme conditions. But many mammals thrive in deserts, including bats, foxes, jack rabbits, kangaroo rats, prairie dogs, wild burros, and wolves.

Jack rabbits have large ears that help keep them cool.

Keeping cool

Desert mammals have special **adaptations** to life in the desert. For example, jack rabbits have large ears that help keep them cool. Blood circulates (moves around) through their ears, helping to shed heat into the surrounding air.

Many desert mammals are **nocturnal.** They remain underground in cool **burrows** during the day, avoiding the hot sun. They emerge at night to find food.

Kangaroo rats never need to drink even a sip of water.

Saving water

All living things need water to survive, so desert mammals have special adaptations to live in such dry conditions. Many get all the water they need from the plants or animals they eat. Kangaroo rats never need to drink water. Their bodies have a special way of making water by combining air with the food they eat.

Camels can go weeks or even months without drinking water. When a camel does find water, it may drink as much as 50 gallons (200 liters) in a

single day. A camel may also store up to 80 pounds (36 kilograms) of fat in its hump, which helps it go for long periods without eating.

Camels also have adaptations for living with sand. A camel's two-toed feet spread out to keep it from sinking into the sand. They also have bushy eyebrows and two rows of eyelashes to protect their eyes from blowing sand.

Desert hunters

Mammals that are **predators** also live in deserts. Desert foxes dig animals out of their burrows. A medium-sized cat called the caracal (*KAR uh kal*) hunts mostly rodents and hares in Asian and African deserts.

Camels can survive in the desert for weeks without eating food or drinking water.

What Mammals Live on Islands?

Islands may contain many different **habitats,** from shorelines to forests to mountains. Small islands may be no larger than a city block and support little life. But some of the larger islands are home to mammals found nowhere else.

Unique island mammals

Many unusual mammals are found only on islands. Rare egg-laying mammals like the duck-billed platypus have survived only on the islands of Australia and Tasmania, where they face little competition. Unusual **marsupials** like kangaroos are also common there.

Ring-tailed lemurs are among the many mammals found only on the island of Madagascar.

The mammals of Madagascar

Madagascar is an island off the coast of Africa where a great number of unusual mammals live. In fact, most of the mammals on this island are found nowhere else on Earth! Monkeylike lemurs disappeared from Africa millions of years ago because they could not compete with monkeys and apes. But lemurs still live on Madagascar, which is free of monkeys and apes.

Madagascar is an island off the coast of Africa.

Big and small

Species of mammals that arrive on islands may become unusually large or small over time. If a species of small mammal arrives on an island, it tends to become larger. There are usually fewer **predators** on islands, so a small mammal that becomes larger may be able to better compete without added risk of being eaten. For example, the giant rat of Flores, an island in Indonesia, is at least twice the size of the common brown rat.

Pygmy elephants on the island of Borneo are smaller than other elephants.

When larger mammals reach islands, they tend to become smaller because there is less land and food available. Smaller mammals need less food, which helps them survive. The pygmy elephants on the island of Borneo are much smaller than other living elephants.

What Mammals Live in Oceans?

The oceans make up the largest **habitat** on our planet, and many mammals live there. Ocean mammals have **adaptations** to life in the water. Instead of ordinary limbs, they have powerful tails and flippers for swimming. Ocean mammals also have streamlined bodies and little or no body hair. This allows them to swim more easily.

Killer whales are actually large dolphins. Like all mammals, they must surface to breathe.

Coming up for air

Unlike fish, ocean mammals cannot breathe underwater. Instead, they must come to the surface to breathe. Dolphins and whales have blowholes on top of their heads. This allows them to draw breath without opening their mouths.

Dolphins and whales

Many **species** of dolphins and whales live in the ocean. These mammals are very intelligent, and many live together in groups. Dolphins hunt together, using **echolocation** to find fish. Killer whales are the largest dolphins and the top **predators** in the ocean. They feed on fish, squid, seals, and other whales.

Most whales feed on the smallest animals, and many lack teeth. Instead, they have hundreds of thin, fringed plates called baleen, which they use like a strainer to remove food from the water. Other whales, like the sperm whale, have teeth and feed on larger **prey.** Sperm whales dive to amazing depths to hunt deep-sea creatures like the giant squid.

Coastal mammals

Mammals like seals and otters are often found hunting fish in waters along the coasts. "Sea cows" like manatees and dugongs spend their entire lives at sea, grazing on water plants.

Manatees are sometimes called sea cows because they graze on water plants.

What Mammals Live in Polar Regions?

The **polar regions** are areas of very cold land and ocean. These areas are so cold that they remain covered in snow and ice all year. Several kinds of mammals live in these extreme **habitats.**

Polar bears have white fur that helps them blend in with ice and snow. The fur also keeps them warm.

The Arctic and Antarctic are very cold regions that lie at the poles.

Where in the world?

The polar regions include the Arctic and Antarctica. The Arctic is the area of water and land around the North Pole. Antarctica is the continent that covers and surrounds the South Pole. Antarctica is the coldest and iciest region in the world, so most plants and animals can't live there. But many seals hunt in the waters around it.

Built for the cold

Mammals survive in polar regions through special **adaptations**. Polar mammals are often larger than other animals, which helps them stay warm. They also have long hair with thick undercoats, and many grow white fur to provide **camouflage**. In addition, they tend to have large feet with furry pads to help them walk on the ice. Some are also protected by a thick layer of fat called blubber.

Crabeater seals are protected from the cold by a thick layer of blubber.

Polar bears are mammals that live in the Arctic, and they have many of these adaptations. They are also skilled swimmers that hunt mainly seals. They do so by breaking into dens and attacking from the sea ice. Whales are swimming mammals that also feed in the polar regions.

Summer living

Winters are long and very cold in the Arctic, but many animals **migrate** there for summer. Large herds of caribou migrate through the Arctic to graze on plants. They make a tasty meal for Arctic wolves, which hunt them.

Other mammals need only leave their underground **burrows** to enjoy summer in the Arctic. Many marmots and other rodents that live in the Arctic **hibernate** through much of the year but are active in the summer. They provide food for wolves and Arctic foxes.

Fun Fact

The narwhal is an Arctic whale known for its unusual spiral tusk. People once sold narwhal tusks as the horns of mythical creatures called unicorns.

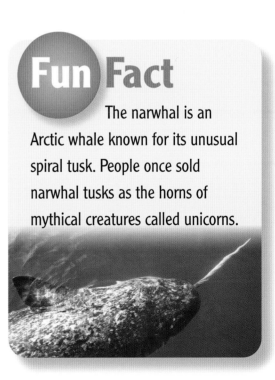

Why Are Some Mammals Endangered?

Tragically, some kinds of mammals are **endangered.** Endangered animals are in danger of becoming extinct (gone forever). Many mammals are endangered, including a wildcat called the Iberian lynx (*y BIHR ee uhn lihngks*) and a dolphin called the vaquita. Some mammals are already extinct, like the Tasmanian wolf and the Chinese river dolphin.

Panda bears are among the many mammals that have become endangered.

Hunting

Some mammals are endangered because human hunters are killing too many of them. Mammals may be hunted for their body parts, which are used to make goods like fine jewelry, art objects, and clothing. Elephants have been hunted for their tusks, and rhinoceroses have been hunted for their horns. Mammals like beavers and tigers have been hunted for their fur.

Some mammals are hunted to provide food, including apes and monkeys. Others are hunted because people consider them a nuisance.

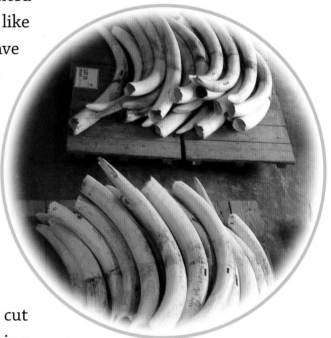

Habitat destruction

Many mammals are endangered because people destroy their **habitats.** In Madagascar, people have cut down more than 80 percent of the forests, threatening hundreds of mammal **species** found nowhere else. **Pollution,** or human-made chemicals that harm nature, threatens mammals in many places.

People have killed large numbers of elephants to take their valuable ivory tusks.

Animal invaders

Mammals may also be threatened by new species that people bring to the area. In Australia, **marsupials** like the toolache wallaby and desert bandicoot became extinct partly because people brought foxes to the country.

Global warming

Global warming is a slow increase in Earth's temperature. Most scientists believe that certain kinds of pollution are causing global warming. Warmer temperatures can damage habitats.

Polar bears are endangered because much of the sea ice they live upon now melts in the summer. Some have drowned trying to swim to distant ice. If Arctic ice melts completely, polar bears may become extinct.

Mountain gorillas are threatened by both habitat destruction and illegal hunting.

How Can We Protect Mammals?

There are many ways that people can help protect mammals and the places where they live. Laws and treaties (agreements between countries) can make it illegal to hunt **endangered** mammals. Governments can establish parks and wildlife refuges to protect **habitats.** Organizations can raise money to protect habitats and help people learn more about endangered animals. Each of us can do our part to help.

People hunt the rhinoceros for the horn on its nose. It is now illegal to hunt rhinos, and many are protected in parks.

Success stories

When people act to protect endangered mammals, those animals often recover. Over the last 200 years, people hunted many whale **species** until the animals were nearly extinct. Now, international treaties forbid most hunting of whales, and whale numbers are slowly increasing.

Making laws

Many countries create laws to protect endangered species. For example, people hunted the gray wolf to near extinction throughout most of the United States. Then the U.S. government made it illegal to hunt wolves in most places, and government scientists planned ways to help wolves recover. Today, the number of gray wolves in the United States is growing.

Protecting habitats

Many countries are trying to protect natural areas that are important to wildlife. In 2008, Australia started one of the largest programs to protect natural resources. The United Kingdom is home to more than 6,500 protected areas.

Doing our part

Each of us can help. Visiting wildlife parks or zoos helps support conservation (the protection of natural resources). People and governments can also work to reduce the amount of **pollution** we cause. This can help slow **global warming** and protect animal habitats. Simply speaking out can help. Let others know about threats to mammals, and tell them it's important that living things be protected.

Park rangers help to protect endangered mammals like mountain gorillas.

By making it illegal to hunt wolves, people have helped these mammals recover.

Activities

Name That Mammal!

Test your knowledge of mammals by taking this quiz. Answers appear in the key at the bottom of this page. **Be sure to use a separate piece of paper to write down your answers.**

1. This mammal is the largest animal that lives on land. It has larger ears than any other animal, and its tusks are the largest teeth.

   a. bear   c. elephant

   b. horse   d. giraffe

2. This mammal is the largest member of the cat family. Its stripes help the animal blend in with its surroundings.

   a. cheetah   c. lion

   b. tiger   d. leopard

3. This mammal has an amazing sense of hearing. It also has good vision. It navigates using **echolocation,** which helps it locate underwater objects in its path.

   a. dolphin   c. seal

   b. whale   d. manatee

4. This mammal is closely related to human beings. It usually walks on all fours, with its feet flat on the ground and its upper body supported on the knuckles of its hands.

   a. zebra   c. wolf

   b. gorilla   d. tiger

5. This mammal is the largest animal on Earth.

   a. elephant   c. bear

   b. giraffe   d. blue whale

Answers: 1. c; 2. b; 3. a; 4. b; 5. d

Endangered Mammals Research Project

Introduction: Many kinds of mammals are **endangered** because of human activities or other causes. The best way to protect endangered animals is to tell other people about the threats to these animals. You can find out more about endangered mammals in your region or country by looking up information in your school or public library.

Materials:
- Poster board
- Markers

Directions:

1. Ask a family member, teacher, or your school or public librarian to help you find information on endangered mammals in your region or country. You may also wish to choose a kind of mammal from another region of the world.

2. Choose a mammal that you wish to learn more about. Write down important information about the mammal and why it is endangered. Questions you may wish to answer include:
   - Where does this mammal live?
   - What is unique about the mammal?
   - What is the mammal's natural **habitat?**
   - What are the main threats to this mammal?
   - How long has the mammal been endangered?
   - What are people doing to help protect the mammal?

3. Draw a picture of the mammal on your poster board. Write down information about the mammal you'd like to share with others. You can present your findings to your class, family, or friends.

Glossary

adaptation; adapted a feature or trait that helps a living thing survive in its environment; suited.

burrow a hole dug in the ground by an animal for shelter; (v.) to dig a hole in the ground.

camouflage (n.) special coloring or texture that helps an animal blend in with its environment; (v.) to look like something else in order to hide.

echolocation a system that certain animals use to find their way. The animals send out short bursts of sound that is too high for human beings to hear. The sound waves bounce off objects, producing echoes. These echoes tell the distance and direction to the objects.

endangered in danger of dying off completely.

equator an imaginary line that goes around Earth's middle.

gland a body part that makes substances the body needs.

global warming the gradual warming of Earth's surface.

habitat a place where a plant or animal lives in the wild.

hibernate; hibernation to spend a period of time in a deep sleep; a condition in which animals seem to be asleep for a long time.

life cycle the stages of development that a living thing passes through.

marsupial a type of mammal that spends its early life attached to its mother's nipple.

migrate; migration to move from one region to another; the movement of animals to a place that offers better living conditions.

nocturnal active at night.

polar regions areas of bitterly cold land and ocean that lie at the northernmost and southernmost parts of Earth.

pollution all the ways that human activity harms nature.

predator a hunting animal.

prey any animal or animals hunted for food by another animal.

reproduce to make more of something.

scavenger an animal that feeds on decaying matter.

species a group of animals or plants that have certain permanent characteristics in common and are able to breed with one another.

territory an area that an animal claims and defends as its own.

vertebrate an animal with a backbone.

warm-blooded having blood that almost always stays about the same temperature no matter what the temperature of the animal's surroundings are.

Find Out More

Books

Exploring the World of Mammals
edited by Nancy B. Simmons and others
(Chelsea House, 2008) 6 volumes
Find out about the body, eating and
breeding habits, habitat, and other facts
for more than 100 mammals worldwide.

**If My Mom Were a Platypus: Mammal
Babies and Their Mothers**
by Dia L. Michels (Platypus Media, 2005)
Learn how 14 different mammals are
born, eat, grow up, and adjust to living in
their world.

Mammal by Jen Green (Dorling
Kindersley, 2005)
This book examines the evolution,
classification, habitat, and geographic
distribution of mammals.

Mammal by Steve Parker and Jane
Burton (Dorling Kindersley, 2004)
Many real-life photographs illustrate the
personal habits, footprints, and unique
traits of various mammals.

The World of Mammals by Sophie
Lockwood and Peter Murray (Child's
World, 2005-) multivolume set
Some of the mammals included in this
series are bats, elephants, chimpanzees,
kangaroos, squirrels, and whales.

Web sites

Animal Cams
http://nationalzoo.si.edu/Animals/WebCams
The National Zoo in Washington, D.C., has
created a virtual zoo by embedding cameras
to videotape 20 animals—mostly
mammals—that live there.

Animals
http://www.oaklandzoo.org/animals/
Click through descriptions and photographs
of all kinds of animals that live at the
Oakland Zoo in California.

**National Geographic Kids: Animals
Creature Features**
http://kids.nationalgeographic.com/
Animals/CreatureFeature
Click on "Mammals" in the menu to learn
about African elephants, black rhinoceroses,
bottlenose dolphins, brown bears, cheetahs,
chimpanzees, coyotes, giant pandas, giraffes,
gray wolves, guanacos, hedgehogs,
hippopotamuses, howler monkeys, koalas,
lions, meerkats, mountain gorillas,
orangutans, and orcas.

U.S. Fish & Wildlife Service: Kids Corner
http://www.fws.gov/endangered/kids/
Find out how you can get involved in saving
wildlife and conserving natural habitats.

Index